Cooking Sous Vide

A Guide for the Home Cook

By Jason Logsdon

Presented By CookingSousVide.com

For more information please contact
Primolicious LLC at 934 West Center St
EXT, Southington, CT 06489.

ISBN: 1449553702
EAN-13: 9781449553708

Table Of Contents

Intro to Sous Vide

Sous vide is quickly becoming one of the hotest new culinary techniques. Here are the ins and outs you need to know to get started.

What is Sous Vide Cooking?

First used in kitchens in France in the 1970s, sous vide is the process of cooking vacuum sealed food in a low temperature water bath over long periods of time. This process helps to achieve texture and tenderness not found with other cooking methods and extends the window of time food can be cooked without being overdone. It has been spreading slowly through professional kitchens and is finally making the jump to home kitchens.

One of the tenants of sous vide cooking is that food should be cooked at the temperature it will be served at. For instance, if you are cooking a steak to medium rare, you want to serve it at 125 degrees Fahrenheit. With traditional cooking, you would cook it on a hot grill or oven at around 400-500 degrees and pull it off at the right moment when the middle has reached 125 degrees. This results in a bulls eye effect of burnt meat on the outside turning to medium rare in the middle and requires exact timing to cook it properly.

Preparing this same steak via sous vide would entail cooking it at 125 degrees for one to two hours. This will result in the entire piece of meat being perfectly cooked medium rare. Since the outside sear adds great flavor and a desirable texture many people will take the finished sous vide meat and quickly grill or sear the outside over very high heat.

There are two basic components to sous vide cooking at home: temperature and time. Each one of these can affect the end quality, texture, and taste of sous vide dishes. Learning to understand how they affect the food is one of the most important things as you begin sous vide cooking.

Temperature

All sous vide cooking is done at temperatures below the boiling point of water and normally not above 185°F. You usually cook the food at the temperature you want it served at, so most settings are between 120°F and 185°F, depending on the food being prepared.

While the range of temperature used in sous vide is much less variable than for traditional cooking, the precise control of the temperature is of great importance.

Time

The use of low temperatures in sous vide cooking requires longer cooking times to achieve the same tenderization as traditional techniques.

Also, your window of time to perfectly cooked food is much longer than with traditional cooking methods because you are cooking the food at the temperature you want it to end up at, rather than a higher temperature. This also allows you to leave food in the water bath even after it is done since keeping it at this temperature does not dry out the food, up to several hours longer for tougher cuts of meat. However, be careful not to take this concept too far as food can still become

overcooked by sous vide, many times without showing it externally.

Temperature and Time Together

The power of sous vide cooking comes from precisely controlling both temperature and time. This is important because of the way meat reacts to different temperatures.

At 120°F meat slowly begins to tenderize as the protein myosin begins to coagulate and the connective tissue in the meat begins to break down. As the temperature increases so does the speed of tenderization.

However, meat also begins to lose its moisture above 140°F as the heat causes the collagen in the cells to shrink and wring out the moisture. This happens very quickly over 150°F and meat becomes completely dried out above 160°F.

Many tough cuts of meat are braised or roasted for a long period of time so the meat can fully tenderize, but because of the high temperatures they can easily become dried out. Using sous vide allows you to hold the meat below the 140°F barrier long enough for the slower tenderization process to be effective. This results in very tender meat that is still moist and not overcooked.

Benefits of Sous Vide

Just like any method of cooking there are many reasons to use the sous vide technique, depending on what you are trying to accomplish.

Moisture

Because food cooked in the sous vide style is vacuum sealed it does not lose much moisture or flavor. The food pouch holds in all the liquid released by the food. This is especially apparent when compared to traditional techniques such as roasting and braising where the meat has a tendency to dry out.

Also, as discussed in the "Temperature and Time Together" section, the low heat used in sous vide prevents the collagen from constricting and forcing out more moisture. Controlling the collagen combined with the vacuum sealing, results in very moist foods.

Tenderness

The sous vide technique allows you to cook tough cuts of meat at an incredibly low temperature, allowing you to tenderize them while remaining perfectly medium-rare. This is very effective for shanks, roasts and other pieces of meat that are typically braised or roasted, but often dry out or get overcooked in the process.

Texture

Using sous vide to cook food also exposes new textures. This is because of two things. First, the vacuum sealing process can make lighter foods denser, like watermelon. Second, the lack of high heat used in cooking can result in silky and smoothly textured food that is impossible to replicate with traditional cooking techniques.

Disadvantages of Sous Vide

Like any culinary technique, sous vide cooking also has its drawbacks. Fortunately, the first two are slowly disappearing as sous vide becomes a more prevalent technique and the third can be minimized with planning.

Information

The first disadvantage is the lack of easily accessible information about sous vide cooking. While there is information out there on websites, forums, books, and magazines, there isn't a single repository you can use to collect it. This has meant a lot of time lost on research before even getting started. This book will be enough to get you started and will also direct you where to find more information as you become more experienced with the technique.

High Cost

The second disadvantage is the high cost of good sous vide equipment. Until recently, the only effective way to do sous vide cooking was by using thermal immersion circulators or thermal circulating water baths, both of which run more than a thousand dollars. Now, some less-expensive alternatives are turning up, such as sous vide cooking controllers, that reduce the cost of getting started to a few hundred dollars. This book covers the different options in the "Sous Vide Equipment" chapter.

Time

The third potential disadvantage is the length of time required to cook some items with sous vide. Even more than braising or roasting, most sous vide cooking requires long periods of time. For many tougher cuts of meat, such as short ribs or brisket, it is recommended you cook them at about 130 degrees Fahrenheit for around 36 hours. Of course, the majority of this time you don't have to do a single thing to them and the energy expended is minimal. There are also several types of sous vide cooking that can be done in 30 to 60 minutes, especially for fish and chicken dishes.

Basic Sous Vide Technique

At the heart of sous vide cooking is a very simple process. While there are variations within each dish, almost every sous vide meal follows the same steps.

Flavor the Food

As in most cooking you first flavor the food. This can be as simple as a sprinkling of salt and pepper or as complicated as adding an elaborate sauce or spice rub. Depending on the type of seasoning it can either be rubbed directly onto the food itself or poured into the pouch with the food.

If you are using a normal home vacuum sealer and want to add more than a little liquid, freeze the liquid before adding it to the pouch. This way the process of vacuum sealing will not suck out the liquid.

Vacuum Seal the Food

Once the seasoning and food has been added to the pouch, suck the air out and seal it closed. Some vacuum sealers have different strengths of vacuum to seal the bag and can be used to affect the texture of some types of food.

Various vacuum sealing options are discussed in the "Vacuum Sealers" section of the "Sous Vide Equipment" chapter.

Heat the Water

Simply bring the water bath up to the temperature you will cook at. Depending on the type of heat regulator, you may be able to have the food in the water while it heats. For others, it is best to pre-heat the water before placing the food in it due to early fluctuations in temperature.

The "Temperature Regulation" section of the "Sous Vide Equipment" chapter discusses the various temperature regulators and water baths available.

Cook the Food

Put the food pouch in the water and let it cook for the amount of time specified in the recipe or on the chart. For items that are cooked for longer amounts of time it can be good to rotate the food every 6 to 10 hours, especially if you are using less precise sous vide equipment.

Finish the Dish

To get a good finish and texture to your food, especially meats, many times it is advisable to quickly sear the meat in a saute pan or with a blow torch. Some meals also call for other methods of finishing the food, such as breading and deep-frying for chicken or mashing potatoes with cream and butter.

Safety Concerns

As with any cooking technique, there are several safety concerns. With sous vide, you should be aware of the potential hazards associated with cooking food in plastic, cooking only at low temperatures, and the freezing and thawing of cooked foods. While most respected chefs and food scientists have no concerns with sous vide cooking when done properly, we encourage you to read up on the issues and make your own judgements about its safety before following any of the recipes in this book. We have gathered a few starting links for you at our website: *http://www.cookingsousvide.com/info/sous-vide-safety-links*.

Sous Vide Equipment

Sous vide cooking doesn't require much equipment, but what it does can vary greatly in cost and function. Here are the main types of equipment needed, and their costs.

Equipment Options

There are two types of equipment you need for sous vide cooking: heat regulators and vacuum sealers. Many people interested in learning sous vide cooking are turned off by the idea of expensive sous vide equipment. While it is true that much of the higher end equipment can get costly, it is still less expensive than many normal kitchen appliances and there are now several less-expensive options available.

We look at the entire range of options you have when purchasing sous vide equipment, from using a pot on the stove with Ziploc bags, to $150 "sous vide controllers", to $1,000 thermal immersion circulators and chambered vacuum sealers.

Just remember, you do not have to bankrupt yourself on expensive sous vide equipment. Start small and test the waters. If you like sous vide cooking then it might be worth spending a little more for some dedicated sous vide equipment.

If you are not concerned with the details of the specific equipment types, feel free to skip ahead to our "Ideal Home Setup" in the next chapter for our complete setup recommendations.

Vacuum Sealers

Note: please see the safety section for information about cooking in plastic.

Vacuum sealing your food in sous vide cooking accomplishes many things. It can change the texture and density of certain foods. It can also make marinades and seasonings absorb more quickly into the food. It also ensures that the water bath is as close to the food as possible and air is not interfering with the cooking process.

There are many ways to seal your food and here are the most popular methods with their advantages and disadvantages, as well as their corresponding prices.

Chambered Vacuum Sealers

The preferred method of sealing your sous vide food is to use a chambered vacuum sealer. These industrial vacuum sealers make use of a large vacuum chamber in which the sous vide food pouch is placed. You then close the chamber and all air is removed and the bag is sealed. These are the kind of vacuum sealers used in professional kitchens.

The biggest benefit of chambered vacuum sealers is that you can easily vacuum seal food that has liquids or marinades in it, something with which the lesser sealers have trouble. Another benefit is that they have more fine-tuned pressure controls, allowing you to manipulate the density of certain foods. However, these abilities come at a high cost and many chambered vacuum sealers are over $1,500.

Both Industria and MSA sell respected chambered vacuum sealers under their brands and the Minipack-torre MVS31 chamber vacuum sealer is highly regarded.

Home Vacuum Sealers

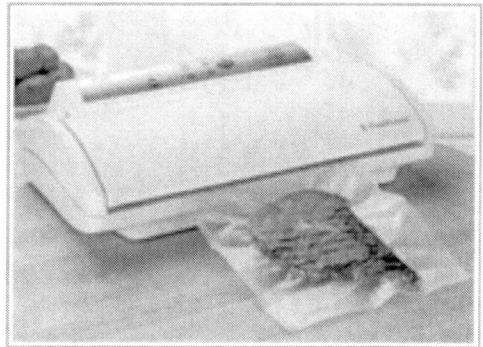

For home cooks the most cost effective method of sealing your sous vide food is to use a standard home vacuum sealer. These vacuum sealers work by inserting the opening of the sous vide food pouch into a small depression in the machine. The sealer then sucks the air out of the pouch and seals it using a heating element.

Preparing food with a standard home vacuum sealer gives you the advantage of sucking all the air out of the bag and ensuring maximum heat transfer between the water and the food. The biggest downside to these vacuum sealers is that the process of sucking out the air also can suck out any liquid in the pouch, making it much more difficult to tightly seal foods with marinades. Many home chefs will still use these sealers and will just seal the bag more loosely if there are marinades or liquids in the pouch, or the liquid can be frozen first.

There are many types of standard vacuum sealers, with Tilia FoodSavers being the most common brand. Tilia FoodSavers make a number of different vacuum sealers, most sold between $100 and $200. Some other less-expensive vacuum sealers are the Rival Seal A Meal and the Deni Vacuum Sealer, though they are usually of less quality than the FoodSavers.

Food Grade Ziploc Bags

If you want to just try out sous vide cooking you can also use food-grade Ziploc bags to seal the food. The Ziploc bags will have more air in them than the vacuum sealed bags and the seal isn't as strong. However, they will work fine for short cook foods, especially if you are just getting started with sous vide cooking and do not want to spend any up-front money.

Food-Grade Plastic Wrap

The other easy method of sealing food for sous vide cooking is to wrap the object in many layers of food grade plastic wrap. This method will allow easy transfer of heat, similar to the vacuum sealed food, but the seal isn't nearly as strong. It will work fine for sous vide cooking for short amounts of time.

Temperature Regulation

Proper temperature control of the water bath is critical to effective sous vide cooking. Temperature fluctuations of a few degrees can drastically change the texture of many dishes.

There are several ways to regulate water temperature and we'll discuss the positives and negatives of the main ones. The techniques range from inexpensive and inexact to incredibly precise with the price tag to match.

Thermal Immersion Circulators

A thermal immersion circulator is a heating device that you put into a container of water that will keep the water at a uniform temperature. Thermal circulators were originally developed for use in laboratory work where precision heating is needed for many tasks.

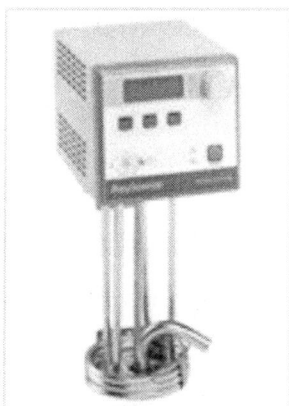

Thermal immersion circulators are probably the best piece of equipment you can get for regulating water temperature in sous vide cooking, but also the most expensive.

How They Work

A standard thermal immersion circulator consists of a heating coil with an attached pump. The heating coil and pump are inserted into a body of water and a temperature is set on the immersion circulator. The heating coil will keep the water at the set temperature while the pump circulates the water to eliminate any hot or cold spots.

Each thermal immersion circulator has it's own margin of error for holding the temperature. Most low-end circulators will hold the water at a +/- 1 degree Celsius, while some high-end circulators can hold the temperature to within +/- 0.01 degrees.

Advantages

The biggest benefit of thermal immersion circulators is their precision. Whether the circulator can regulate the heat from within 1 degree celsius or 0.01 degree, it is more than acceptable for perfect sous vide cooking.

Most thermal immersion circulators can also be attached to the edge of a normal kitchen pot, making them very convenient to use in sous vide cooking at home.

Disadvantages

The biggest issue with thermal immersion circulators is the high cost of purchasing them. They routinely sell new ones for $800 to $1,500, and used ones are $200 to $600 which is pretty expensive for a piece of home kitchen equipment, especially one specific for sous vide cooking.

A minor negative of thermal immersion circulators is the evaporation due to not having a sealed lid. You can use foil or saran wrap to try and seal it better but you will still suffer some evaporation. This normally isn't a big deal unless you are using a 24+ hour sous vide preparation and then you will have to remember to occasionally add water.

Where to Buy

Probably the best known brand of thermal immersion circulators is Brinkmann, who makes the Lauda immersion circulators. PolyScience also makes well known circulators. As of the writing of this book, Sur La Table also recently launched their own line of immersion circulators manufactured by Julabo, both of which normally have high quality equipment.

You can also look for used thermal immersion circulators on eBay and from scientific lab resell sites. If you do buy a used thermal immersion circulator, be sure to clean it properly since you never know what chemicals were used in it previously. For that reason, some people refuse to cook with previously used immersion circulators; do so at your own risk.

Thermal Circulating Water Bath

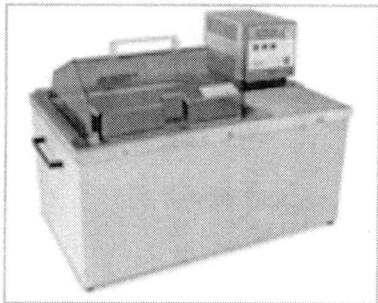

The other heavy duty way to regulate water temperature in sous vide cooking is through the use of a thermal circulating water bath. These devices are similar to the thermal immersion circulators except they come in their own enclosed container for holding the water. Like the immersion circulators, water baths were originally developed for the scientific lab where maintaining precision temperatures can be critical.

How It Works
A normal water bath consists of a lidded container of water with a built in thermal immersion circulator or other heating and circulating device. The container holds the water, and in sous vide cooking the food in a pouch, while the heating unit regulates the temperature of the water and removes all hot and cold spots.

Advantages
Since the circulating water bath has a sealed container it can help reduce evaporation during very long sous vide preparations. They also more easily keep the temperature of the water constant throughout the sous vide process since it is enclosed, requiring less electricity.

Every circulating water bath has its own margin of error for holding the temperature. Most low-end circulators will hold the water at a +/- 1 degree Celsius, while some high-end circulators can hold the temperature to within +/- 0.01 degrees. Either of which is more than enough precision for sous vide cooking.

Disadvantages
Much like the thermal immersion circulators, the largest issue with circulating water baths is their expense. They are also in the $800 to $2,000 range for new equipment.

Where to Buy

PolyScience makes well known thermal water baths. At the time of this writing Sur La Table also released a new line of circulating water baths.

You can also look for used thermal water baths on eBay and sites that resell scientific lab equipment. If you do buy a used thermal water bath, be sure to clean it well since you never know what chemicals were used in it previously. For that reason, some people refuse to cook with previously used water baths; do so at your own risk.

Sous Vide Cooking Controller

While thermal immersion circulators and thermal circulating water baths are the undisputed leaders of precision temperature control they are out of the price range of many home cooks. Some companies are finally addressing this fact and coming out with interesting ways of regulating water temperature for much less money.

One of the best combo systems is the sous vide cooking controller. This device is pretty simple in principal and is used with a rice cooker, crock pot, slow cooker, or other similar device many home cooks have on hand.

How It Works

The sous vide cooking controller is basically a plug with an automated on / off switch that is controlled by a thermometer. Here are the four steps to using it:

1) Take your slow cooker, crock pot or rice cooker and fill it with warm water.
2) Plug your slow cooker into the outlet on the sous vide cooking controller and turn it on to its highest setting.

3) Put the thermometer attached to the cooking controller into the water in the slow cooker.
4) Set the cooking controller temperature display to the temperature you want to maintain during the cooking process.
5) Finally, put the vacuum sealed food into the crock pot and let it cook for the specified time.

The sous vide cooking controller then turns the crock pot on and off to keep the temperature of the water in the slow cooker at a stable temperature.

Advantages
The low price tag is probably the biggest benefit to using a sous vide controller. Most are between $110 and $180, depending on the control desired. Both Auber Instruments and SousVideMagic sell similar types of sous vide controllers that are easily within the price range of most home cooks.

Sous vide controllers are used with your existing crock pots, slow cookers, and rice cookers, check the sous vide controller for specific brands supported. This is definitely a nice convenience and helps save money.

Most sous vide controllers can regulate the temperature to within 1 degree celsius, which is adequate for most sous vide preparations.

Disadvantages
The biggest downside of sous vide controllers is the lack of precision. While most of the producers claim their controllers maintain steady, even heat, they aren't as precise as the more expensive thermal immersion circulators or the thermal water baths, especially in short time frames.

However, most people, including us, feel that the sous vide controllers do have enough precision for the home cook to produce excellent results in sous vide cooking.

Where to Buy
SousVideMagic
(http://freshmealssolutions.com/index.php)

makes a very popular sous vide controller and has very good customer service, tell Frank that CookingSousVide.com sent you. Auber Instruments also sells sous vide controllers for comparable prices.

Sous Vide on the Stove

The cheapest, and least precise, way to do sous vide cooking is directly on your stove. It only requires a stove, a thermometer, some hot water, some cold water, and a good amount of patience.

How It Works

Fill a pot with luke warm water. A larger pot is better since it will hold its temperature when the vacuum sealed sous vide packet is added and it will also be more stable while cooking.

Place a thermometer in the water, preferably a digital meat thermometer with a long cord since that way the thermometer is convenient and easy to read.

Add either hot water or cold water to bring the pot to the desired temperature. You can also briefly turn a burner on or add ice cubes if you need to move the temperature quickly.

Add the vacuum sealed sous vide packets and bring the water back up to the temperature you need.

Leave the food in the water for as long as the recipe says. Be sure to regularly check the water temperature to make sure it is where you want.

Advantages

The only real advantage of doing sous vide on your stove is that it is very cheap and doesn't require any special equipment.

Disadvantages

Cooking sous vide this way is very imprecise. No matter how diligent you are about checking the water temperature and adjusting it, it will definitely fluctuate by several degrees, and most likely 5-10 degrees. This can play havoc with the texture and doneness of certain types of sous vide food.

It also takes a lot of work to maintain a specific water temperature. You have to constantly be by the water, checking the temperature and adjusting it. This is fine for short cooking sous vide items like fish or some vegetables but for a longer term item it quickly becomes impractical.

Tips for Sous Vide on the Stove

Use a wooden spoon to regularly stir the water, making sure to go up and down as well as side to side. This will help to better even out the temperature of the water.

A larger pot will also hold its temperature better and have a more stable temperature.

Common Sous Vide Setups

With all the options for sous vide equipment available it can be hard to determine how to get stared. Some setups run thousands of dollars while others are only a few hundred. Here are a few of our recommended sous vide setups and the associated costs with each.

Ideal Home Sous Vide Setup

This home sous vide setup has everything you need to create great sous vide results in your own kitchen. It's by far the most cost efficient method for the home cook and requires very little effort to set up and use.

While this method can cost several hundred dollars to set up from scratch, many cooks already have some of the equipment on hand. Most of the equipment in this setup can also be reused for non-sous vide purposes so they are not just a single-technique item.

If you are looking for an inexpensive but effective sous vide setup then this one is for you.

Food Sealing

Home vacuum sealers can be found for $125+ and they make sous vide cooking much easier. While they fall short of the power and features of a chambered vacuum sealer they are about a thousand dollars less expensive and bring enough features to make it worth while. There are also many more reasons to get a vacuum sealer. We recommend the FoodSaver V2440, it's not the most recent version but it is consistently the highest rated and is less-expensive than the newer versions.

Water Bath

For this home sous vide setup the best water bath is a typical self-heating device, rice cookers are the best but crock pots also work very well. As long as the chamber is big enough for the size of food you will normally be cooking then you should be fine. If you currently own a rice cooker or crock pot then go ahead and use it, if not then I recommend starting with a rice cooker because it has better distribution of heat.

Temperature Control

The most cost-effective way to control temperature is with a sous vide controller. There are many different brands but SousVideMagic has a good reputation and focuses almost exclusively on sous vide cooking, it is also what I personally use at home. The sous vide controller works by measuring the temperature of your water bath and turning your heating device (the crock pot or rice cooker) on and off to maintain a consistent temperature. I've had great results with this even for short ribs that were cooked for over 48 hours.

Cooking the Food

With this sous vide setup there are only two "hands-on" cooking moments required. The first is to pre-heat the water bath, this will help to keep a steady temperature in the water bath due to the way the sous vide controller works. The second is during long-cooking dishes when you occasionally rotate the food in the water bath, about every 6-10 hours if possible. That is all the effort you have to expend to have very high-quality sous vide food.

Total Cost

Vacuum Sealer: $150

Sous Vide Controller: $150
Crock Pot / Rice Cooker: $150
Total Cost: $450 for a complete sous vide set up, assuming you don't have any of the equipment already.

Advanced Sous Vide Setup

For the ultimate in home sous vide the advanced setup will give you the precision and control you need for perfect sous vide cooking. However, this power does not come cheap. The equipment used in the advanced setup is generally outside the scope of this book but we can make some general recommendations.

Food Sealing

As discussed in the equipment section, chambered vacuum sealers are the sealing work-horses of professional kitchens. They offer great control over the vacuum and pressure applied to the foods and well as the ability to easily vacuum seal liquids. Industria and MSA are well known companies with respected chambered vacuum sealers; the Minipack-torre MVS31 chamber vacuum sealer is also highly regarded.

Water Bath and Heat Control

For heat control we recommend the PolyScience 7306C immersion circulator which is accurate to within 0.09°F for temperatures up to 300°F. Since the immersion circulator can be attached to any pan we recommend using any pan you have around, or even a deep hotel pan.

Cooking the Food

Depending on the type of pot used you'll probably suffer some evaporation so the water should be checked and refilled during long cooking times. Aside from that, this setup provides hands-off cooking.

Total Cost

Vacuum Sealer: $2,085

Sous Vide Controller: $969

Total Cost: $3,054 for a complete advanced sous vide set up.

Cheap Sous Vide Setup

One of the big misconceptions about sous vide cooking is that you have to spend thousands of dollars to do it. While it is possible to spend that much money you can also get a very good sous vide set up for much cheaper, or even for free.

This cheap sous vide setup can be applied to many dishes that don't require long amounts of cooking time such as many vegetables or most types of fish. However, you can't use this setup for most types of meat because of the constant work required to maintain the proper temperature and the fluctuations in temperature.

Food Sealing

For the cheap sous vide setup you can wrap the food in food-grade plastic wrap several layers thick, or even use a food-grade Ziploc bag with all the air removed. If you already have a vacuum sealer such as a FoodSaver around then definitely use it to seal the food.

Water Bath

The cheapest way to set up a water bath is to use a pot of water on your stove. A large pot is easier to work with than a small pot since it maintains its temperature better.

Temperature Control

Working with a thermometer it is pretty easy to maintain a temperature within a few degrees to either side of your ideal temperature. Leaving the stove on low, or turning it on and off, and adding ice cubes or cold water in small amounts allows you to keep the water temperature relatively stable. It won't stay within the .1 degree range that many devices can maintain but for short amounts of time it will do just fine.

I recommend using a meat thermometer with a cord, that way it's easy to keep it out of the way while you regulate the water temperature.

Cooking the Food

Once you put the food in the water, try to maintain the temperature that you are aiming for as closely as possible and you'll need to cook most dishes for 15 to 20 minutes, or up to an hour. Anything longer begins to become unmanageable.

Total Cost

About $25 for a thermometer if you don't already have one, otherwise it is basically a free method to try sous vide cooking.

While this method of cheap sous vide is more time and effort intensive than other methods it's a great place to experiment and see if you want to invest the few hundred dollars to move up to a basic "hands-off" set up with a crock pot / rice cooker and a sous vide controller that we recommend in the Ideal Home Sous Vide Setup.

Tips and Tricks

While the majority of sous vide cooking is relatively simple, there are still some things to keep in mind that can increase your chances of success. Here are some of the more important ones.

Flavor

Always Salt and Pepper

Salt and peppering your food before vacuum sealing it will only enhance the flavors of the finished meal. It's recommended for almost every dish to add salt and pepper before cooking it.

Easy on the Spices

Because of the length of time sous vide cooking requires, especially for the tough cuts of meat, and the effects of the vacuum seal, spices can come across much stronger than they would in a roast or braise. It's better to err of the side of less and re-season after cooking than to try and eat a dish that tastes like raw garlic.

Turn to the Powders

Using fresh herbs and spices instead of dried is normally a good idea when cooking. However, with sous vide it can be better to use the dried powders in some cases. This is especially true for things like garlic and ginger because the raw form of both can sometimes create a bitterness in the final dish.

Give it Some Smoke

If you are preparing a BBQ-style dish it can help if you smoke the meat before sealing it. Even 30-60 minutes in the smoker can add a lot of flavor to the final dish. It's normally better to smoke the food before cooking it as opposed to afterwards.

Cheat on the Smoke

If you don't have a smoker or the time to smoke your food there is a quicker way to add some smokiness. Instead of smoking it you can add a small amount of Liquid Smoke to the bag prior to it being sealed.

Don't Forget the Brine

Even though sous vide cooking traps most of the moisture and flavor in the food it never hurts to brine your chicken or pork first as it will result in even more tender and flavorful meat. For an easy brine mix 1 cup of salt, 1/2 cup of sugar, and 1 gallon of water, bring to a boil for 5 minutes, cool completely, then fully submerge the meat in it for 4-12 hours depending on the size of the meat. You can also add in spices or herbs to add additional flavor, like rosemary, thyme, peppercorns, or bay leaves which will transfer through the brine into the meat.

Hold the Booze

Alcohol based marinades are a classic way to cook, from bourbon in BBQ sauce to red wine in braises. However, when it comes to sous vide you can run into trouble with a marinade that has alcohol in it. Because of the low temperature and the sealed bag the alcohol will not evaporate off which can lead to a dish that has a harsh alcohol flavor instead of the mellow undertones.

Freeze it First

Many sous vide recipes call for a marinade or sauce to be sealed into the pouch with the food. This is fine with a chambered vacuum sealer but for normal home sealers it can be problematic since the sealer will suck the liquid out. One method to get around this is to first freeze the

liquid then vacuum seal it while it is "solid". The ice will defrost as it is cooking and still be very effective.

Zip it Up

Some liquids will not freeze so to get them sealed you can first put the food and the liquid into a Ziploc bag, then vacuum seal that in a standard food pouch. It will not maintain as good of a vacuum but it will work pretty well.

Tailor to Your Guests

Since sous vide dishes can be cooked in individual pouches it allows you to tailor the portions to who is eating them. For instance, if someone is alergic to pepper or spices you can do one pouch without the pepper and the others with it.

You can also use two or three different seasonings in a batch of sous vide by sealing them seperately. Then you can let everyone mix and match and eat the ones they prefer.

Cooking

Don't Stuff The Pouches

In order to ensure proper cooking it's important to make sure the width of your pouches are relatively even. Don't force in extra food or layer the food in the pouches. It's better to use multiple pouches with a single layer of food than one large pouch. Most recipes assume a single layer of food when determining the cooking time.

Remove the Fat

Since sous vide cooking does not get up to high temperatures it does not render fat nearly as well as other cooking techniques. When it comes to dishes cooked over a long period of time, such as short ribs or a roast, be sure to remove any extra fat from the meat before cooking it. This will result in a much leaner and more tender meat with a lot better texture.

Turn Up the Heat

Most meat cooked sous vide should be done with very un-fatty cuts. However, if you find yourself with a more fatty cut you can turn the temperature up to about 150°F which will help break down the collagen without drying it out completely. The same cut of meat cooked at 130°F will actually be tougher because of the excess of collagen.

Preheat the Water

Preheating your water is very important for dishes that are cooked for a short amount of time. The temperature of the water can fluctuate wildly during the first 30-60 minutes and can adversely affect the outcome of your dish if it is only in the water that long. For sous vide dishes that are cooked for five hours or more it isn't as important but preheating never hurts.

Heavy on the Water

This is an important tip, especially for items cooked over a short period of time. Even if you preheat the water, when you put the colder food into the water bath the temperature will drop and the heating element will go into overdrive to bring it back up to temperature. The more water you are cooking in the less the temperature will drop. It can also help to let you food sit out for 15-30 minutes to come up to a higher temperature so the change in the water won't be as severe

Time Saving

Make and Freeze Your Own Steaks

Because of the ability of sous vide to transform tough cuts of meat into very tender "steaks" some people will cook a chuck roast with sous vide, cool it, then slice it into 1" thick slices and freeze them. When they're ready to eat they remove a slice from the freezer and sear on the grill or in a pan. It can be a good way to transform a cheap cut of meat into the equivalent of a much more expensive steak.

Bring Out the Blow Torch

If you have a pastry blow torch you can use it to sear the finished meat instead of pan-frying or grilling. Be warned though, it can be hard to sear chicken with a torch without burning it.

Fast Preheating

A simple way to preheat the water in your sous vide bath is to fill it 1/2 way full with room temperature water, then heat 3-4 cups of water in the microwave. Then you can fill the water bath the rest of the way with a mixture of the hot water and the room temperature water, watching the thermometer to make sure the temperature stays near where you need it to be.

Recipes

Please read the recipes all the way through before starting on them. Many of the dishes require finishing touches once the food is taken out of the water bath and sometimes these steps start while the food is still in the water.

These recipes are also general guidelines so feel free to experiment with them in any way you would like to.

Rosemary Short Ribs

Time: 36-48 hours

Temperature: 133°F

Serves: 4

2-3 pounds short ribs, preferably
lean ribs

2-3 sprigs of rosemary

2 tablespoons Worcestershire sauce

2 tablespoons butter

1 tablespoon vegetable or canola oil

1/2 teaspoon pepper

Pre-Bath
Pre-heat the water bath to 133°F.

Add the ribs, rosemary, worcester
sauce and pepper to the pouch and
seal. Cook the ribs for 36 to 48 hours
at 133°F.

Rotate the meat pouches in the
water bath every 6 to 10 hours if
possible.

Finishing
Heat a pan over medium-high heat.

Remove the ribs from the pouch,
place on a plate, and cover with foil.
Discard the rosemary and pour the
liquid from the pouches into another
small saucepan and place on the
stove over medium-high heat to

reduce and thicken, stir in two tablespoons of butter.

Blot the ribs dry with paper towels or a kitchen towel. Add canola or vegetable oil to the pan on the stove. Lightly salt and pepper the outside of the ribs. Once the oil just begins to smoke, add the ribs to the pan and quickly brown the outside, about 1 to 1 1/2 minutes, flip the ribs over and repeat on that side.

Remove the ribs and serve with the reduced sauce. These ribs go great with mashed potatoes, mixed vegetables, or a nice salad. For a smokier flavor you can also quickly grill the short ribs over high heat instead of pan frying them.

Pot Roast

Time: 36-48 hours

Temperature: 130°F

Serves: 8

3-4 pounds of beef chuck roast or pot roast
3 tablespoons canola, olive, or vegetable oil
1 medium onion, coarsely chopped
3 cloves garlic, diced
4 carrots, peeled and cut into 1" pieces
5-10 fingerling potatoes, cut into 1" cubes
1 bay leaf
2 sprigs of rosemary
3 sprigs of thyme
1/2 cup red wine
1 cup beef stock
1/2 cup flour
1/2 cup cold water

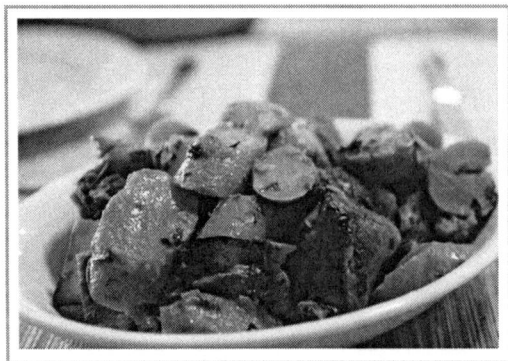

Pre-Bath
Pre-heat the water bath to 130°F.

Prepare the meat by trimming off any excess fat and then slicing into 2" slabs. Salt and pepper the meat then vacuum seal it and place in the water bath. Let it cook for 36-48 hours.

Rotate the meat pouches in the water bath every 6 to 10 hours if possible.

Finishing
About an hour before you want to serve the roast, heat the oil over medium to medium-high heat in a pot or a deep pan. Place the onions and garlic in the pan and sweat them for about 10 minutes until the onions turn translucent. Add the carrots, potatoes, bay leaf, rosemary, thyme, red wine, and beef stock. If the vegetables are not covered add enough water to just cover them. Lightly simmer for 50 minutes, until the carrots and potatoes are tender. Then remove the vegetables from the simmering liquid, reserving the

liquid in the pan, and set aside the vegetables under foil.

Remove the meat pouches from the water and carefully cut open, pouring the liquid inside into the reserved vegetable liquid. Place the slabs of meat on a plate under foil.

Mix the flour with the cold water and whisk until there are no clumps. Slowly whisk 1/2 of the flour-water mixture into the pot of vegetable liquid and bring to a boil. Continue whisking in more until the sauce is the consistency you like.

Serve the meat with the vegetables and the gravy on the side. The pot roast is great when served with a fresh baguette, sourdough bread, or dinner rolls.

Mango-Chipotle Beef Ribs

Time: 48 hours

Temperature: 135°F

Serves: 3-6

For the Ribs
2-3 pounds beef ribs

Salt

1/2 teaspoon pepper

For the BBQ Sauce
Or use your favorite bottled version

2 mangos, diced

1 onion, diced

6 cloves garlic, minced

Several chipotles in adobo, to taste

1 cup ketchup

1/2 cup coffee

1/4 cup Worcestershire sauce

2 tablespoons lemon juice

1/4 cup apple cider vinegar

1/3 cup packed brown sugar

1 tablespoon Dijon mustard

2 teaspoons kosher salt

Pre-Bath
Pre-heat the water bath to 135°F.

Salt and pepper the beef ribs and then vacuum seal them.

Cook the ribs for 36 to 48 hours at 135°F turning the pouches in the water bath every 6 to 10 hours if possible.

Finishing
At least an hour before you are planning to serve the ribs you should make the BBQ sauce. Heat 2 tablespoons oil in a pot over medium-high heat and saute the onion and garlic about 3-6 minutes, until they turn translucent. Place all the remaining ingredients in the pot and simmer gently for 20-30 minutes. Blend the BBQ sauce with a

blender or preferably an immersion blender until it is smooth. Be careful not to fill the blender too full since the liquid will expand. Return to the stove and let simmer until it is the consistency you desire. You can do this up to two days ahead of time and keep it refrigerated.

Heat a grill to high-heat. You won't be cooking the ribs long on it, just searing them, so use the hottest setting.

Remove the ribs from the pouch, blot dry with a paper towel, and place on a plate. Smear a light layer of the BBQ sauce on the ribs then place on the grill and cook for 1 to 2 minutes, until the sauce starts to blacken and the ribs have a good sear on them.

Remove the ribs from the grill, smear another light layer of BBQ sauce on them and serve with the rest of the sauce on the side.

These ribs go great with fresh corn, a cucumber-tomato salad, or corn

bread. For milder ribs you can use less chipotle or a bottled BBQ sauce you prefer.

Buttermilk Fried Chicken

Time: 1 hour

Temperature: 141°F

Serves: 4

4 chicken breasts

4 lemon slices

4 sage leaves

3 cups flour

2 tablespoons garlic powder

2 tablespoons paprika

1 teaspoon chipotle or cayenne powder

3 cups buttermilk

Canola oil for frying

Pre-Bath

Pre-heat the water bath to 141°F.

Place each chicken breast in a pouch with a sage leaf and a lemon slice. Salt and pepper the chicken breasts and then vacuum seal them.

Cook the chicken breasts for around an hour at 141°F.

Finishing

Near the end of the cooking time, set up the batter stations and the oil. Combine the flour, garlic powder, paprika, and chipotle powder into a shallow dish and mix thoroughly. Pour the buttermilk into a separate shallow dish. Fill a deep pot with canola oil to a depth of around 3" and heat to 365 to 375 degrees, or use a deep-fryer if you have one. Be sure the oil fills the pot less than halfway since it will expand when the chicken breasts are added.

Remove the pouches from the water bath and take the chicken breasts out and pat each one dry with a paper towel. One at a time take each breast and dredge them in the flour mixture, then dip it in the buttermilk, and finally dredge it in the flour one more time. Set aside on a plate and repeat for all the chicken breasts.

Add the chicken breasts slowly, one at a time, into the hot oil and cook until the coating is browned and very crunchy. Remove from the oil, sprinkle with salt and pepper, and drain on a wire rack.

These fried chicken breasts are great with fresh corn, mashed potatoes, or even macaroni and cheese.

BBQ Chicken Thighs

Time: 2 hours

Temperature: 160°F

Serves: 4

6 chicken thighs

1/2 teaspoon pepper

1 tablespoon garlic powder

3 sprigs of thyme

1-2 cups BBQ sauce

Pre-Bath

Pre-heat the water bath to 160°F.

Trim most of the excess fat off of the thighs. Evenly distribute the garlic powder over them, then salt and pepper each one. Place the chicken thighs in the pouches with one half of a thyme sprig per thigh then vacuum seal them.

Cook the chicken thighs for around two hours at 160°F.

Finishing

Heat a grill to high-heat. You won't be cooking the thighs long on it, just searing them, so use the hottest setting.

Remove the thighs from the pouch, blot dry with a paper towel, and place on a plate. Smear a light layer of the BBQ sauce on the thighs then place on the grill and cook for 1 to 2 minutes, until the sauce starts to blacken and the thighs have a good sear on them.

Remove the thighs from the grill, smear another light layer of BBQ sauce on them and serve with the rest of the sauce on the side.

These thighs go great with watermelon, green beans, or wild rice.

Maple Glazed Pork Chops

Time: 12 hours

Temperature: 131°F

Serves: 4

4 pork chops, bone removed

4 tablespoons maple syrup

Pre-Bath
Pre-heat the water bath to 131°F.

Salt and pepper the pork chops and place into pouches with one tablespoon of maple syrup per pork chop. Vacuum seal the pouches.

Cook the pork chops for around 12 hours at 131°F.

Finishing
Heat a grill to high-heat. You won't be cooking the pork chops long on it, just searing them, so use the hottest setting.

Remove the pork chops from the pouches and blot dry with a paper towel or dish towel. Place the chops on the grill and cook for 1 to 2

minutes per side, until they get a
good sear and grill marks develop.

These pork chops are great with a
summer salad, corn bread, green
beans, or mashed potatoes.

Smoky Lamb Chops

Time: 3-4 hours

Temperature: 131°F

Serves: 4

2-4 pounds lamb chops

1 tablespoon sweet paprika

1 tablespoon garlic powder

1 teaspoon pepper

4 sprigs of rosemary

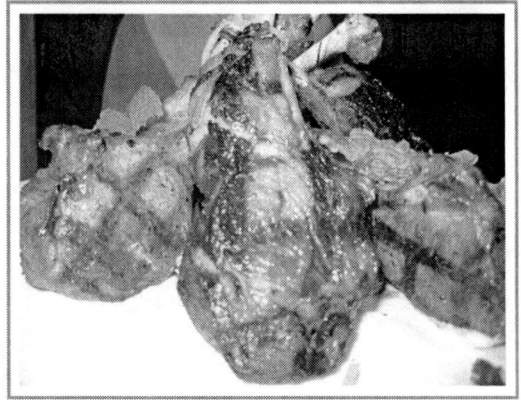

Pre-Bath
Pre-heat the water bath to 131°F.

Evenly distribute the garlic powder and paprika over the lamb chops, then salt and pepper each one. Place the chops in the pouches with the rosemary evenly divided among them then vacuum seal closed.

Cook the lamb chops for three to four hours at 131°F.

Finishing
Heat a pan over medium-high heat.

Remove the lamb chops from the pouch, place on a plate, and cover with foil.

Discard the rosemary and pour the liquid from the pouches into a small saucepan and place on the stove over medium-high heat to reduce and thicken, stir in two tablespoons of butter.

Blot the lamb chops dry with paper towels or a kitchen towel. Add canola or vegetable oil to the pan on the stove. Once the oil just begins to smoke, add the chops to the pan and quickly brown the outside, about 1 to 1 1/2 minutes, flip the lamb over and repeat on the other side.

Remove the lamb chops and serve with the reduced sauce.

These chops go great with mashed potatoes, green beans, or a salad. For an even smokier flavor you can also quickly grill the lamb chops over high heat instead of pan frying them.

Halibut

Time: 15 minutes

Temperature: 135°F

Serves: 4

4 5-6 ounce halibut filets

1/2 tablespoon onion powder

1/4 teaspoon pepper

1 lemon

1-2 tablespoons olive oil

Pre-Bath
Pre-heat the water bath to 135°F.

Evenly distribute the onion powder on the halibut filets then salt and pepper each one. Add the halibut pieces to the vacuum pouch and seal. Cook for about 15 minutes at 135°F.

Finishing
Remove the halibut from the pouches, place on a plate and drizzle with the lemon juice and olive oil.

This halibut goes great with green beans, rice, or a light salad.

"Almost Sushi" Salmon

Time: 20 minutes

Temperature: 104°F

Serves: 4

2 salmon filets, skin removed

2 tablespoons soy sauce

1 teaspoon wasabi, wasabi paste, or horseradish

1 teaspoon ginger powder

1/4 teaspoon pepper

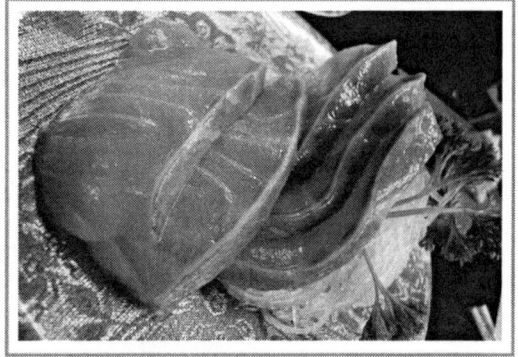

Pre-Bath

Pre-heat the water bath to 104°F.

Take two pouches and to each one add 1 of the salmon filets and half of the soy sauce, wasabi, pepper, and ginger. Seal and cook for about 20 minutes at 104°F.

Finishing

Remove the salmon from the pouches and place in the refrigerator for at least 1 hour, and up to four hours, to cool. Then slice thinly and serve with rice, stir-fried vegetables, or a cucumber and tomato salad.

Rosemary-Almond Green Beans

Time: 30 minutes

Temperature: 185°F

Serves: 4 to 8

2 pounds fresh green beans

2 tablespoons salted butter

2 rosemary sprigs

1/2 teaspoon pepper

1/4 cup sliced almonds

Sea Salt (or table salt)

Pre-Bath

Pre-heat the water bath to 185°F.

Trim off the stem end of the green beans. Then add the green beans, butter, rosemary and pepper into a pouch and seal it. Make sure the beans are in a single or double layer, it may help to use multiple pouches.

Cook the beans for around 30 minutes at 185°F.

Finishing

Take the beans out of the pouches, remove the rosemary, and put them in a serving dish or on the plates. Sprinkle the sliced almonds and sea salt over the beans and serve.

These beans go great with a roast or grilled chicken or steak.

Eggs and Toast

Time: 60 minutes

Temperature: 150°F

Serves: 4

8 eggs, in the shell

2 tablespoons butter

2 tablespoons fresh tarragon

Parmesean cheese

4 slices of bread, ideally crusty French or sourdough bread

Pre-Bath

Pre-heat the water bath to 150°F.

Place the eggs into the water bath in their shells, being careful not to break them. Let cook for 60 minutes.

Finishing

Right before you take the eggs out, toast the slices of bread and lightly butter them.

Take the eggs out of the water bath. Crack the eggs open and place 2 on each piece of toast. Sprinkle with the tarragon leaves and parmesean cheese then salt and pepper.

These eggs are also great with hash browns, home fries, bacon, or other breakfast foods.

Roasted Garlic - Basil Mashed Potatoes

Time: 60 minutes

Temperature: 185°F

Serves: 4 to 6

2 pounds Yukon Gold potatoes

6 tablespoons butter

1/2 teaspoon pepper

1 head of garlic

1 bunch of basil, cut into thin strips

1/2 cup heavy cream or whole milk

Pre-Bath
Pre-heat the water bath to 185°F.

Cut the potatoes into cubes no large than 1 1/2" wide. Add the potatoes and butter into a sous vide pouch along with a little pepper. Make sure the potatoes are in a single layer, it may help to use multiple pouches. Seal the pouches and place in the water bath.

Cook the potatoes for around 60 minutes at 185°F. The longer you cook them the more tender they will be so if you prefer less tender potatoes then 30-45 minutes is about perfect.

Finishing
40 to 50 minutes before the potatoes are done take the head of garlic and cut off the entire root end, leaving

the rest of the head intact. Drizzle the cut portion with olive oil and sprinkle with salt. Wrap the head in foil and place in the oven, or toaster oven, at 400 degrees.

30 to 40 minutes later, or 10 minutes before the potatoes are done, take the garlic out of the oven, unwrap it and let it cool.

Take the potatoes out of the pouches and place in a large mixing bowl. Squeeze the cooled head of garlic over the bowl and the roasted cloves should come right out. If you are using a large head of garlic, or would prefer less garlicky potatoes then do not use the entire head. Pour in the heavy cream or milk. Mash the mixture together using a potato masher, dough cutter, or large fork. Be sure not to over mash it or the potatoes will begin to get sticky and tough. Once they are mashed to a nice consistency add the basil strips, salt and pepper to taste, and mix lightly.

These potatoes go great as a side dish for a roast or a braise.

Time and Temperature Charts

One of the more interesting aspects of sous vide cooking is how much the time and temperature used can change the texture of the food. Many people experiment with different cooking times and temperatures to tweak dishes various ways.

The numbers below are merely beginning recommendations and are a good place to start. Feel free to increase or lower the temperature several degrees or play around with the cooking time as you see fit.

Meat (Tender Cuts)

Tender meat doesn't benefit as much from sous vide as tough cuts or some fish but it can still produce wonderful results and ensure perfectly cooked dishes every time.

Meat (Tender)	Time
Sirloin	Rare: 125°F for 45 minutes
	Medium Rare: 139°F for 45 minutes
Tenderloin	135°F for 45 minutes
Filet mignon	135°F for 45 minutes
Rib-eye, T-Bone	126°F for 45 minutes
Porterhouse	130°F for 1 hour
Beef Sausage	145°F for 1 hour
Pork Sausage	160°F for 1 hour
Pork Chop	131°F for 12 hours
Pork Tenderloin	140°F for 2 hours
Veal Breast	140°F for 10 hours
Veal Tenderloin	141°F for 30 minutes
Lamb Chop	131°F for 3 hours
Leg of Lamb	135°F for 3 hours
Lamb Saddle	140°F for 2 hours

Meat (Tough Cuts)

Tough cuts of meat benefit more from sous vide than probably anything else. The ability to hold the meat above the tenderization temperature but below the drying out temperature results in unique textures and incredible tenderness. Most of the following times can be changed by several hours with minor loss of texture or flavor.

Meat (Tough Cuts)	Temperature and Time
Short Ribs	135°F for 48 hours
Pork Belly	180°F for 8 to 12 hours
Spare Ribs	141°F for 24 hours
Baby Back Ribs	170°F for 12 hours
Beef Ribs	135°F for 48 hours
Pork Ribs	Quick: 176°F for 12 hours Slow: 155°F for 24 hours
Pork Shoulder	155°F for 24 hours
Chuck Roast	131°F for 30 to 48 hours
Flank Steak	130°F for 24 hours
Bottom Round Roast	128°F for 10 hours
Chuck / top round	131°F for 24 to 48 hours
Pork Roast, Boston Butt, Picnic Roast	Quick: 176°F for 8-12 hours Slow: 155°F for 24 hours
Beef Brisket	146°F for 48 hours
Rack of Lamb	131°F for 12 hours

Poultry

Cooking poultry with sous vide can result in some interesting textures and also ensures moist, flavorful meat, something that can be hard to achieve with traditional cooking methods.

Poultry	Temperature and Time
Chicken Breast	140°F for 60 to 90 minutes
Chicken Thigh	160°F for 2 hours
Chicken Legs	167 for 60 minutes
Turkey Breast	140°F for 7 hours
Turkey Sausage	145°F for 1 hour
Duck Leg	178°F for 8 hours
Duck Breast	141°F for 25 minutes
Rabbit Leg	136°F for 50 minutes
Egg	Over Easy: 144°F for 1 hour Over Hard: 150°F for 1 hour

Fish and Shellfish

Certain fish cooked sous vide take on unique textures that can't be achieved with traditional cooking methods. Salmon is especially interesting when cooked at low temperatures. Adding buter to the pouches also simulates poaching fish in butter and results in great flavor.

Seafood	Temperature and Time
Cod	140°F for 15 minutes
Halibut	135°F for 15 minutes
Lobster	140°F for 25 minutes
Monkfish	Quick Monk: 140°F for 12 minutes Slow Monk: 119°F for 1 hour
Salmon	Rare: 104°F for 20 minutes Medium Rare: 130°F for 15 minutes Medium: 140°F for 15 minutes
Salmon Confit	104°F for 20 minutes
Sea Bass	130°F for 30 minutes
Shrimp	138°F for 20 minutes
Striped Bass - Belly	127°F for 35 minutes
Tuna	130°F for 20 minutes

Vegetables

Sous vide vegetables can be cooked to the exact tenderness you prefer so feel free to experiment with the times listed below until you find the tenderness you enjoy most. Several studies have also shown that vegetables cooked by sous vide retain more of their nutrients than vegetables that are steamed or boiled.

Vegetable	Temperature and Time
Beets	180°F for 40 minutes
Broccoli	185°F for 20 minutes
Brussels Sprouts	180°F for 40 minutes
Carrots	185°F for 35 minutes
Cauliflower	185°F for 15 minutes
Fennel	185°F for 45 minutes
Green Beans	185°F for 30 minutes
Pea Pods	185°F for 20 minutes
Potatoes	Regular: 185°F for 45 minutes Mashed: 185°F for 60 minutes
Radishes	185°F for 25 minutes
Turnips	185°F for 30 minutes

Fahrenheit to Celsius Conversion

All temperatures in this guide are given in Fahrenheit, however some sous vide equipment only works in Celsius. To convert from Fahrenheit to Celsius take the temperature, then subtract 32 from it and multiply the result by 5/9:

(Fahrenheit - 32) * 5/9 = Celsius

We've listed out the temperatures from 37°C to 87°C which are the most commonly used range in sous vide.

Celsius	Fahrenheit	Celsius	Fahrenheit
37	98.6	64	147.2
38	100.4	65	149.0
39	102.2	66	150.8
40	104.0	67	152.6
41	105.8	68	154.4
42	107.6	69	156.2
43	109.4	70	158.0
44	111.2	71	159.8
45	113.0	72	161.6
46	114.8	73	163.4
47	116.6	74	165.2
48	118.4	75	167.0
49	120.2	76	168.8
50	122.0	77	170.6
51	123.8	78	172.4
52	125.6	79	174.2
53	127.4	80	176.0
54	129.2	81	177.8
55	131.0	82	179.6
56	132.8	83	181.4
57	134.6	84	183.2
58	136.4	85	185.0
59	138.2	86	186.8
60	140.0	87	188.6
61	141.8	88	190.4
62	143.6	89	192.2
63	145.4	90	194.0

Resources

Sous vide is a very complex process and there is much more to learn about it besides what has been covered in this book. Here are some resources to help you continue to learn more.

Further Reading

Websites
A Practical Guide to Sous Vide Cooking
Written by Douglas Baldwin, this is one of the best guides available for the scientific principles behind sous vide cooking.

http://amath.colorado.edu/~baldwind/sous-vide.html

Sous Vide: Recipes, Techniques & Equipment
A very long forum string from eGullet, about 98 pages long at this time that covers almost everything you need to know about sous vide if you have the time to look through it all.

http://forums.egullet.org/index.php?showtopic=116617&st=0

Cooking Sous Vide
This is the main website I contribute sous vide articles to. We update it regularly with new recipes and news from around the sous vide community.

http://www.cookingsousvide.com/

Sous Vide Safety Links
Our collection to links about sous vide safety.

http://www.cookingsousvide.com/info/sous-vide-safety-links

Books
Under Pressure: Cooking Sous Vide
By Thomas Keller

A beautifully presented book about very refined sous vide cooking.

Sous Vide
By Viktor Stampfer

A collection of some of Viktor's best sous vide recipes. Be sure to get a copy that is in English, as many copies are not.

Sous-Vide Cuisine

By Joan Roca

From the authors: "we propose our book, as a progression that involves three concepts of sous-vide: Storage, Cooking and Cuisine." Be sure to get a copy that is in English, as many copies are not.

On Food and Cooking

By Harold McGee

This is the ultimate guide to the scientific aspects of cooking.

Acknolwedgements

Sous vide is a brand new field for the home cook and the effort of several people has been instrumental in moving it forward. Nathan Myhrvold helped to almost single-handedly push sous vide cooking to home cooks through his research and contributions to the eGullet thread as well as his interviews in the mainstream press. Douglas Baldwin wrote his incomparable guide to the science behind sous vide and the research he's done around it. Frank Hsu from Fresh Meals Solutions has been developing sous vide products specifically for the home chef and trying to educate people about the benefits of using sous vide cooking at home. There are also many home cooks out there contributing to the sous vide community through their personal blogs sharing recipes, successes and failures in sous vide. Also, the professional chefs who have been using and perfecting this technique for the last three decades including Thomas Keller, Viktor Stampfer, and Joan Roca.

This book would not have been possible without all of their hard work and the information they have made available to the community.

Photo Credits

Many of the photos are excellent pictures and representitive of what your food will look like when following the recipes. Thanks to the following people for making their work available to the public for re-use.

Cover - Orange and Fennel Short Ribs: Jodi Logsdon

Rosemary Short Ribs: http://www.flickr.com/photos/arndog/

Pot Roast: http://www.flickr.com/photos/glenmaclarty/

Mango-Chipotle Beef Ribs: http://www.flickr.com/photos/galant/

Fried Chicken: http://www.flickr.com/photos/arndog/

BBQ Chicken Thighs: http://www.flickr.com/photos/dongkwan/

Maple Glazed Pork Chops: http://www.flickr.com/photos/stevendepolo/

Smoky Lamb Chops: http://www.flickr.com/photos/jeffreyallen/

Halibut: http://www.flickr.com/photos/clairity/

"Almost Sushi" Salmon: http://www.flickr.com/photos/pittaya/

Rosemary-Almond Green Beans: http://www.flickr.com/photos/pong/

Roasted Garlic Mashed Potatoes: http://www.flickr.com/photos/habesha/

Eggs and Toast: http://www.flickr.com/photos/stine1121/

About the Author

Jason Logsdon is an avid cook and web developer. He is a co-founder of and main contributor to CookingSousVide.com. He can be reached at jason@cookingsousvide.com.

LaVergne, TN USA
09 August 2010
192651LV00003B/30/P